THE DEVIL KNOCKS BUT GOD ANSWERS!

The Devil Knocks But God Answers!

Henry L. Bryant Jr.

Henry L. Bryant Jr.

THE DEVIL KNOCKS BUT GOD ANSWERS!

- A TRUE STORY -

This book is dedicated to everyone that has, is, or will go through trials and tribulations that seem impossible to overcome.

Contents

1	Accident Day	1
2	My Eyes Are Opened	4
3	Finally Admitted	7
4	The Procedure	11
5	Hard to Remember	14
6	How Much More Pain	16
7	Homeward Bound	19
8	Controlling My Feelings	22
9	Back On My Feet	25
10	Walk Before You Run	28
11	Just the Beginning	31
12	Acknowledgements	33
13	Synopsis	35

1

Accident Day

~

Accident Day – 10/30/2016

    It was a beautiful Sunday evening in Savannah, Georgia, not too hot, not too cold, that just right weather. I decided to ride my motorcycle out to Tybee Island with my wife on back. We drove out to the beach enjoying the open air and each other's company, looking around at the marshlands and blue sky. Reaching the beach, we walked around in the sand for a little then sat in the swing set, looked out at the waters, and relaxed. We were in the moment being in love and not stressing about anything to come. After a while, we decided to head back home to get dinner and then get back into the routine of the work week; got to love it. Little did I know my life was destined to change dramatically in the next hour. Almost home, and we noticed traffic ahead is slowing down; it appears an accident occurred in the lanes coming onward. We were headed toward it, back into town. So right as we pass the accident, I'm almost at a stop, and out of nowhere... from oncoming traffic... I see a white F-150 truck crossing the median heading right at us. With barely any time to react, I turned the front end of my motorcycle to avoid him hitting us from the side.

Even though I swerved, he hit the front of my motorcycle throwing me into his truck. I never passed out and felt my body hitting his truck as I was airborne. I believe my body knocked my wife into the air because we both went flying, but she wasn't hit by the truck as I was. I land on my back in total shock like, what the hell just happened. I cried out, "Oh my God! Oh my God! Somebody help! Where's my wife? Where's my wife? Is she okay? I can't see my body." My head was pointed straight up, and I couldn't move. People rushed out from their cars screaming, "Don't move! Call for help," while I kept screaming, "Is she okay!" Finally, voices say ,"She is fine. You are hurt very bad and losing a lot of blood, and your leg is very bad." Someone said, "We need to put a tourniquet around your leg so this may hurt." I felt no pain; I just started saying, "Lord, forgive me," because I thought I was going to die. I was yelling, "Tell my wife I love her, tell her I love her, tell my family I love them." Someone held my hand and said, "I'm praying with you for God to protect and heal you." I'm not sure how long I was on the pavement, but it was long enough for the sun to burn my skin from the hot pavement. The ambulance comes, and I hear, "We are going to take you first, because you are in a severe condition." They put me in the ambulance while I'm yelling to my wife, "I love you" and "I'm sorry," and still praying to God. During that ride to the hospital, I literally was seeing my life flash before my eyes: visions of people, family, fun times. I thought this was only movie talk, but it isn't, it's real. When we reached the hospital, I really felt my life was coming to an end; my breathing started slowing as they rushed me off the ambulance into the hospital. My vision was blurry since the accident, and I never saw anyone's face from the time the accident happened. Unable to focus, as I'm being rushed down the hallway, I remember seeing the lights from above; no other images were available. I hear the confusion and panic of the workers as I'm being rushed to the operating room. Again, never able to focus on a face, I thought that was it for me. I was placed on the table and then told to count to ten; and then I was out...

2

My Eyes Are Opened

~

My Eyes Are Opened

Honestly, I wasn't even sure what time of day it is at this point as my eyes open. I look around the room and see my family and wife and her family. So glad to be alive, I can't even put it into words. Of course, I'm not all the way alert; due to the fact, I'm still pretty much under the influences of all the meds. So I'm tired, but just woke up. Yes, I'm all bandaged up, and right now have no pain, I guess I'm still in shock and disbelief. Everyone starts to talk to me and ask if I remember anything, and they let me know what the doctor said about the steps needed for recovery. I was so glad to see everyone. As tears of joy run down my face, I smile and crack jokes with the family about saving my wife's life. She's sitting in a wheelchair while I'm laid out in the bed. At the moment, neither of us knew the extent to our injuries, but I knew for sure I wasn't in a position to walk or move around. After sometime, my wife and family departed so she could go home and get cleaned up while the nurses gave me more medicine to go back to sleep. The next morning, I wake up to the doctor giving me the full report to my injuries, the worst being my leg. In addition to that, I had a fractured pinky, my hip was dislocated, I had road rash pretty bad, broken ribs, and some other cuts and bruises. The bone in my leg broke through my skin in multiple places. I was not too familiar with all the technical terms, but let's just say my right leg was jacked up. I had pins in my foot, seemed like pins in my ankle, screws in my foot and up through my leg, and screws in my thigh on that same leg. It looked like my leg and foot was caught in a giant bear trap or something. Never saw anything like it, and it was heavy due to the fact I wasn't a small tiny guy and my leg was swollen. It was a form of an external fixation device used to keep fractured bones stabilized and aligned. At first sight, the external fixator to me was what I thought would save my leg, and hopefully, I would go back to normal. The doctor comes in and informs me due to the severity of my injury to my leg they were going to transport me to Augusta Medical University from Memorial Hospital because they have some of the best orthopedic surgeons available. My family is informed, and now I'm being packed in another ambulance to make a two-and-a-half hour drive, not knowing what to expect when I arrived. Mind you the first time I had ever ridden in an ambulance ever was like a day ago, and I was in shock, but now I'm alert and haven't had my pain meds before leaving. I was told the hospital would be awaiting my arrival. My family went to prepare to come to Augusta and bring some of my personal items from home later after I got settled there. Now back to the ambulance, ahhhh, worst ride ever! There's no way to strap me down in the back, I can't sit up, I'm on a stretcher bed, and I have a cage on my leg that pulls with pain as we hit bumps or make turns. It was the bumpiest ride I've ever been on. At one point, I thought the driver was hitting potholes on purpose. All I could do was pray and ask God to take my mind off the pain and time passing slowly and help me relax until we get there. Finally after 2 ½ hours and about 10,000 pot holes and 400 turns, they are wheeling me into the Augusta hospital. I'm ready because pain is at an intolerable level now. The drivers roll me inside, and guess what, the workers act like they didn't know I was coming or had even got word to be ready to give me pain medicine. At this point, I'm in tears due to the miscommunication and pain as I'm just laying on the stretcher in one of the hallways...

3

Finally Admitted

~

Finally Admitted

In the Bible, we read about how God has his angels all over the world aiding his children and even appearing to humans who are unaware of their heavenly status. Because he is all-knowing, he always has them placed in the right places at the right time. I witnessed this when I was being admitted to the new hospital. As I was transported from the ambulance, this young lady at the front desk seeing the pain, frustration, sadness, disappointment, anger and whatever that was on my face, began to talk to me, reassuring me that she would solve whatever problems prevented me from being in a room already. She single-handedly was able to get things moving and soon has managed to have me placed in a room. Throughout the encounter, she remained so compassionate and so thoughtful in attempting to make me as comfortable as possible while speaking in a soothing, understanding tone of voice. Once I was in my room, she also came in and apologized for the way things had gone and for the pain that she could tell I was in. I'm convinced that in an effort to distract me from my current circumstances and pain levels she began to remind me how good God is. To this day, I'm unsure of how she knew that her words would resonate with me or even that I wasn't an unbeliever. All my reasoning has convinced me that she must have been especially sent from God just for me just for that time. Whatever the reason, she prayed with me that day like she knew me all my life. Her efforts, most importantly the prayer, settled my pain to a tolerable level. Amazingly, this happened without any medications being administered. God is amazing in how he works, who he uses to perform his will, and when he chooses to accomplish miracles. He is the great Physician and is the only doctor who truly has mastered the human body, both mentally and physically. Although he chooses to allow doctors to receive praise for healing the sick, God is the doctor, writing prescriptions and enabling human doctors to heal the sick. Feeling the relief, I continued to pray and talk with her till the doctors had verified all the necessary paperwork was completed and proper medications were given to alleviate what had been excruciating pain. This woman, who I had never met and who knew nothing about me, was able to sense that I knew God as she saw the God within me. Because she was prayerfully working that day, God showed her what to do and even guided her mouth in what to say. She listened to God's directions, and although this was not part of her job description, it was part of God's plan and his position sits higher than all things. He will perform his plan, no matter what.

After getting settled, all the doctor's come in and confirmed my injuries. They advised me of upcoming procedures along with the overall plan for recovery. They let me know of any possible problems that could occur with each surgery and their contingency plan for each scenario. They assured me they would exhaust every option in order to save my leg. This was their greatest concern as it was in the worst shape out of all my injuries. Because of the trauma of the accident, blood clots had formed in my leg. They explained that these blood clots hindered many of their normal methods for treating my leg injuries so that I could make a full recover.

Their first choice was to flush the clots out, but this was soon removed as an option because with it I would bleed to death from my leg being exposed in places where my bones tore through the skin as a result of the compound fracture. The worst case scenario that everyone sought to avoid was amputation of my leg and immediately. While I listened to their discussions and nodded at the right spots, my brain was spinning with all the options and terms these doctors threw around like anyone should know them and had thought of these choices before. In my head, I was like ,ohhhhhh no, no, no, absolutely not. *God, I know you didn't bring me this far to lose my leg. How would that fit into any plan you want for me. I know you'll help them find a way to save it.* Once they neared a stopping point in their conversation, I pleaded with these doctors, who held my recovery in their hands and who could alter my life course with their decisions, that they try everything else possible before amputation was even made a discussion. I was assured that "we are the best here and we will collaborate and brainstorm on what possible routes we could take to lead to a full recover". Relieved, I was like cool, as long as we stay away from amputation village, we are good.

Days have passed at this point, and I'm in no better of a situation than when I was transferred there. Restless nights grew into stressful days of sitting awaiting possible good news. Every morning around 6 a.m., the doctors would announce their entrance with a knock on my room's door. This signaled the start to my day and was preceded with a horrible feeling in the pit of my stomach. All the anticipation had been built up from the day before when they had entered my room in their morning rounds. Emotions up and down, this became routine, and I grew to dread the time after the doctors left because of the one conversation in the mornings and the waiting all day: wondering, *damn, what will they say tomorrow, will I hear good news, bad news or more of the same.* I became tired of hearing the phrases: "We are working on it; we're putting our heads together." In the meantime, I'm trying to have faith, keep faith, be strong, stay strong, and it's so hard. It's so hard to stand firm in faith when everything seems to go wrong, especially when you don't see it coming or see a way out of the situation. I had it in my head that God didn't want me to lose my leg, and I wasn't going to accept that as a possibility. To my way of understanding, there was nothing good that could possibly come out of the amputation outcome. I did recognize that since the accident and move to the new hospital I had talked to God more than I ever had before. Not that I didn't talk to him before, but lately, it was like he's the only one that exists because he is the only one that will see me through this. He's also the only one who can fix my leg – of that, I'm convinced.

Finally, after hearing the doctor's opinion, I resigned my will to entertain the thought of amputation, and in my head, I accept the fact that losing my leg may be a possibility. I began to play the what-if scenarios in my head. What if – they have to amputate what will my life be then. What will I do for work, how will I function on my own? My mind became busy with all the different outcomes that I kept hidden deep inside. Although I had started processing this worst-case scenario, I wasn't giving up yet and didn't tell anyone my thoughts. One morning, during the doctors morning chat, they told me that they may have found a way to get the blood clots out my leg while still being able to save it. The surgery required would be a major surgery, and like any other surgery, the risks were there. I didn't care; all I heard was, "We have found a way… to keep your leg." After listening to all the possibilities and risks, I enthusiastically said, "Yes, let's do it! Thank you, I knew you would find a way." With my spirits lifted, the day seemed to go much faster in anticipation. But wait, while running all the tests to prepare for the surgery, they noticed a devastating problem…

4

The Procedure

~

The Procedure

My 2nd scariest and most terrifying moment in my life happens only about 24 days after my 1st moment which was my devastating accident on October 30, 2016. Now on November 22, 2016, I get the word that I am left with no other choice than to have my leg amputated. Because of my condition, the procedure would need to take place the next day which is the twenty-third of November. *Damn*, I thought, *not right before Turkey Day. God, this has to be a joke*, my mind initially was convinced that this was an ironic turn of events, if not a borderline unfunny joke. I'm in Augusta far away from Savannah, *maybe someone's filming a prank show here with me as the star and any second they will pop out from behind the curtain telling me this is all a crazy prank*. But reality set in, when they brought me authorization papers to sign. Now, my time was filled with meeting with the surgeons to go over the whole procedure. To be honest, I don't recall any emotions at that time: no anger, no sorrow, no anticipation, no anything. I guess this is what is known as being in the state of shock, if not unreal. I went through the motions of signing the paperwork not even reading what they said completely and not being able to hear them as they talked to me. I recall a sense of numbness and detachment from what was going on right around me. When faced with life-altering decisions, I simply did what was expected of me rather than dwelling on the outcome. What good would have been accomplished by my analysis of these events? If anything, this would have resulted in depression and despondency.

Not too long after the doctors left, I let myself think about what was about to happen. Once the realization set in, I began to break down then. It was as if I had remained strong just long enough to ensure there were no witnesses; then, the flood of emotions burst forth. "No, no, no, no, this can't be happening!" as I yell out, "but I can still wiggle my toes, that has to mean something." I feel a slight sensation in my foot. *Oh God, please don't let this happen to me. Why me... why me... why me... this isn't happening. Please don't let this happen. I can't; I just can't.* I laid there and just cried, tears running down my face, eyes beginning to swell from just pouring out my emotions. My family was in the room, but there was nothing anyone could say that made me stop. No matter how good, correct, or accurate their sentiments may have seemed; none of it helped. All I could think was, *I'm going to lose my leg.* Thirty-four years old, having my legs all my life, now, I'm in a hospital bed, crying because they are going to amputate my leg due to someone else's negligence that led to the accident that fateful day. I couldn't eat, not because of restrictions with the procedure coming up, but because of the what the procedure involved; ahh, mainly my leg.

The time has come, and the transporters are standing in my doorway saying, "Mr. Bryant, it's time." My family stands around me as my mom prays before I take, what seems to be, that last ride. Her prayer asks for God's guidance to the surgeons' hands, strength for me, and most importantly, God's will to be performed. I try to be strong for my family and for my wife, but as soon as I'm out of their sight, the tears began to roll again. This time there was no need to try and wipe them away in an effort to appear strong and brave. Instead, I just let them fall as I look up to heaven and pray that God give me strength in answer to my mother's prayers. Later I found, that my family and many others, also continued to pray during this time. Together our prayers went up to God's ears, and I'm sure that the requests mirrored my own that day. *God*, I began, *I know I'm not perfect, but please if I must go through with this, help me, don't leave me, hold my hand. I can't do this on my own.* The tears rolled more and more as we went through doors and elevators all the way into the operating room. When I got to the operating area, all the nurses and workers down there were trying to cheer me up because I had been done there a few times prior. For those instances, I was in great spirits and had joked with them trying to bring some humor to my day and theirs. Just like this time, everyone was friendly and engaged me in personal conversation. But this time although it was helping, it also made it worse because now we're minutes away, and my composure has dissolved, I can't hold anything back now. Those tears just kept coming all the way until they put the mask over face and put me to sleep...

5

Hard to Remember

~

Hard to Remember

The surgery was a success, or so the doctors said, but I couldn't be happy at the moment because my right leg has just been amputated below the knee. I'm laying there in the post-surgery area in shock still. Did I look at my leg, you ask? At first no, I just laid there, not moving and stared at the sheets, because I could see my left foot but not my right. I'm not sure how long it took before I looked under the sheet, and honestly, I don't remember if I looked myself or laid there till the doctor or nurse came by and pulled it back first. Either way, my initial reaction was no reaction. My tears had all been spent before the surgery so for now I had no more tears, no words, no nothing. After recover, they told me, "It's time to go back to your room; your family and wife are waiting on you and will be so glad to see you." As I'm being transported back to my room, I look up to the ceiling, not saying anything, just looking as we pass under the lights. Once they rolled me back into the room, everyone starts to smile and thank God that I made it through, and again, I try to be strong, but my emotions were still just on a break.

While they all talk quietly, I watch television as I lay there, not thinking about anything at all. Looking at my leg along with everyone else as I hear their words of, "You're strong." "You're going to make it through this; you've come this far." "We don't know why this happened, but it had to happen, and God will see you through this." I begin to talk a little, and the nurses come by to fill me in on other procedures that are scheduled. Soon, the doctors come into my room to check on me and confirm the necessary upcoming procedures. Pain was kicking in by then so I was brought my doses of painkillers and quickly drifted off to sleep as I hear the laughter and sounds of my family thanking God that I made it through.

Later, when I woke up, someone was sent to my room to talk with me about the future steps. The thing that I remember the most was discussing one day getting a prosthetic. This remained in the future, but at the moment, I was excited for that possibility. During the surgery, they had been able to remove the blood clots in my leg, but I also still had two areas where skin was missing. Down the road, I would need a skin graft to cover those two spots. But for now, I would have yet another device hooked up to my leg. When does it end, I wondered? When will it be the last surgery, the last doctor visit, the last procedure, the last hospital stay? Now since the huge external fixator (my leg) is gone, and below the knee, my leg was gone, here comes into play the wonderful wound vac. Mind you, all this equipment and procedures are brand-new to me so I have no idea what to expect or what the overall procedures involve. Only thing I could think of was, *how much pain will this contraption cause me and for how long. I just want to be done with all this.* The only explanation that they gave me was, "Well, this is the next step we have to do" and "It won't be painful…"

6

How Much More Pain

~

How Much More Pain

I tell you, you hear sayings and quotes all the time, but they take on new meaning when you are the one they are quoting these too. Wow, that's all I can say. God never puts more on us than we can bear is a common saying that I'm sure we've all heard. I was told this more times than I remember, and I found this to be true as well: God made humans extremely strong. Now that I think about it, if I had a choice, I may have chosen child birth over these painful ordeals I went and am currently going through. I've never felt pain in so many different ways physically in my life.

The accident, being hit and thrown in the air, the ride in ambulance with fixator on my leg, the removal of the external fixator and days before that, the wound vac, changing of the suction areas and phantom pains is all enough to bring you to your knees and tears to your eyes. All pain, all horrible, all have different levels summing up to the feeling of just make it stop. When I had the external fixator on, moving was just out the question because you literally have screws and pins going through your leg. So if it's bumped or pulled in anyway, the pain radiated in ways that you don't want to ever feel. I found no real way to get comfortable with that on. Add to this, the uncomfortableness and awkwardness when you have nurses trying to wash you and needing x-rays done with it on. It required two or more people who would lift up on it at the same time to avoid pulling too hard against your leg. I remember so vividly the day they took this cage off my leg. I was told, "Oh, we are going to take this off, and it won't hurt, and besides, we will have the nurses give you meds so it won't be bad at all." Let me tell, you now, if they say it's not going to hurt; it's going to hurt like hell so make sure they give you any and all meds possible before they start. I asked if this was normal to take this off bedside and not be put to sleep. They both told me it was standard procedure and the nurse will give you meds for pain after. Now I'm scared, nervous, terrified, all at the same time; the crew that's responsible for taking it off walk back in with rods in their hands. I was looking at their equipment like damn; they brought things to work on me like an old box Chevrolet Caprice. My wife was like they look like they are about to put a bike together not fix your leg. Do you know I laid there while they unscrewed the pins in my foot and leg? My thigh was dripping blood as they are removed, and all I hear them saying is "you're doing great," "keep breathing," and "almost done." I can't even put into words how painful this was and how traumatizing this has been for me. I was in so much pain as they left the room saying, "We will get the nurse." When the nurse came in, she said, "They should have let you take the meds before they did this." SMH, *you got to be kidding me*, I thought. Keep in mind this had to be done to help prepare for my surgery for amputation.

Now I have this wound vac on that covers two extremely large parts of my leg to keep the areas from getting infected where all my skin was missing. Soon as I begin to think this isn't too bad, they told me, "We need to change the padding." *Um what was that? excuse me.* Yes, every two to three days, the padding needed to be changed to keep the area clean. Knowing the pain this caused, they let me go for maybe four to five days between changing, and the first three times they did this they took me down to a surgery area and put me to sleep so I wouldn't have pain from the process. Okay, so now they were saying it can be done bedside by the nurse while I'm awake. They explained how it would go, and I cringed when I heard those dreaded words. "It's not going to hurt." Hell, I don't know about that since I was put to sleep the first three times so it must hurt when done. Well I was right, again, hurt like hell. As they changed the pads, they were stuck to the open flesh in each spot. It felt like someone taking a knife, stabbing you with it, then dragging it through your flesh till the very end of the area. Pouring this medical solution to loosen the gauze as they went did little to ease the pain and speed up the process. It is hard to say if it helped at all, but it didn't seem like it helps much. It was enough pain to make me feel light headed and praying for it to be done. *Please God, let this be the last spot*, I cried out, looking up at the ceiling in hopes to witness a miracle that it would all be over.

On top of all these things, you have phantom pain which makes it feel like you still have your whole limb but you don't. Imagine your foot or hand hurting, but you can't see it or grab it or tuck it or rub it. Everyone has their limits, and everyone's experiences if similar to mine are still very different. But on this I think we can all agree that IT SUCKS! Thank God, my phantom pain was under control due to the meds I was given daily. I think God was like, "He's close to his all-he-can-bear limit so let's give him a break, at least for now. He's going to need his strength for the rest of this journey..."

7

Homeward Bound

~

Homeward Bound

Now it's been almost two-and-a-half months of being in hospitals. I had been moved in and out of rooms, given x-rays after x-rays to evaluate the process. I grew to anticipate the routine of daily vitals, routine lab work, testing, and physical therapy. During this time, I remained immobile with not even a glimpse of the outside world or feeling fresh air on my face. After what seemed an eternity, they give the blessed words that I am being released. I remained composed as I processed that simple statement, but internally, I was celebrating, *Well, it's about damn time.* I don't know what to expect once I get out. One thing I knew to expect was to get out of here. One would think that I would have thoughts of would I be able to pick up where I left off or would everything have changed since the accident? Instead, I had no thoughts about life on the outside or what to come or how I will feel about all that's happened. I was just excited to be able to go home and try to get back to life in the outside world. I had to leave with the wound vac in place and was given the chance to find a doctor in Savannah to finish up my last surgeries that would be needed. This was so that I wouldn't have to return there. Sounds like a plan to me, my parents contacted one of my cousins, and she was able to get help and find a doctor and schedule appointments. Another item marked off of our growing checklist. But all that mattered was I was going home!

One leg, crutch, and a wheelchair later, I was rolling down the long hallway to the exit to leave the hospital to head home with my bags and whatever other items that belonged to me in tow. Saying my goodbye and waving PEACE OUT to everybody, tears crept up in my eyes. This time, they were tears of joy this time, not sadness. Once inside the car, all I could do is look out the window at the hospital as it grew smaller in the distance. As we pulled off and away, I was just thanking God because I didn't think I would make it this far. Every procedure, every doctor conversation, every decision were a step along the way to the end goal of recover. Each brought pros and cons with them not making anything easy. I looked out that window the whole time, and as we got further away, reality slowly started kicking in. I'm headed home… I lost my leg…What to do next? Will I ever walk again? Just thoughts after thoughts after thoughts, I tried listening to music, but at a certain point, you start to hear nothing, and you just stare out into the world scared, nervous, anxious; so many emotions.

Nevertheless, I was happy and tried to look at the positives in my situation. It's hard not to worry about everything when you reach a point you feel like you can do nothing. We stopped at one my many favorite restaurants and ordered food through the drive-thru. I had been eating hospital food(which was not too bad) for two-and-a-half months; so at this point, everything looked and sounded good to me. I enjoyed the rest of the ride home and actually was able to calm down a little and clear my head of all the what-next scenarios of the future. There would be plenty of time to think about those; for now, I simply enjoyed this new-found freedom. Besides, everyone was so happy I was headed back home instead of being two-and-a-half hours away from my hometown...

8

Controlling My Feelings

~

Controlling My Feelings

    Laying in my bed day in and day out, sometimes I sleep, sometimes I'm sitting staring straight into the air. With my thoughts all over the place, I had so many questions still, so many concerns about my future. I directed my questions which mostly involved "why me" toward the only person that knew the answer. Why was I singled out to suffer this accident? Why had I gone through all the procedures just to lose my leg?. I started talking to myself and talking to God, trying to sort through all my questions, all my thoughts. *Lord*, I began, *I know I haven't been perfect, but I was trying to live the life of a Christian. I didn't make it to church every Sunday, but I believe in you, and I try to treat everyone right and love everybody.* Many days were spent just crying and fussing at God and being angry and disappointed in my situation. So many thoughts of confusion as to why my life has gone down this road of heartache and so much pain. I know right now of plenty of people that I thought maybe deserved to have this happen to them because of all the wrong they participated in. I thought, *Man, this should have been for someone out there being reckless not respecting life,* whether on a motorcycle or not. My mantra continued with reckless abandon repeating: why, why, why, why...

One day after all my complaining and all my questioning was finished, through all my anger, through all my sadness, I finally stopped questioning, and God answered me. At that moment when my mind seemed to be clear, he answered, "Why not you, my son?"

Now when you hear God talk to you plainly, it can seem as if someone is physically speaking to you in the room at that moment. Sometimes you have to look around to make sure because it seems so real and audible. God continued to say, "I know your pain and all about your suffering, I know how you feel, and I know you have questions and concerns, but I want to tell you through it all I'm still right here with you. Through everything that has happened from day one, I've been there; I have never left you. I have plans for you, and you may not understand it now, but faith will lead you to all your answers one day. You see if I didn't have something magnificent planned for you in your life, your time would have been up that day. But you have more work to do, and you'll understand it by and by." Now when the average person tells you something, we tend to question what we don't understand, what we can't predict, and what we just can't seem to comprehend. But when God speaks to you, the only response is Thank You. Now thank you has many forms; thank you for life, strength, guidance, understanding, saving grace, for my past, for my present, for my future. So no matter how hard it may seem to get, remember God has not left you to fight your battle alone. Keep faith and keep moving no matter how fast or slow you may think things are going, keep moving. God also told me that my struggles were not over yet. He said, "You are still going to be faced with things in your life, and you may feel like you just can't take it anymore. Remember I saved you from that accident and brought you to this point so just keep faith and remember who I am.

It's so easy to have faith and speak it when you haven't gone through anything in life, but when you're put to the test, where will your faith lie? God won't put more on us then we can bear.

9

Back On My Feet

~

Back on My Feet

All my praying and anticipation for the day that I would walk again is finally here. Through all the pain, trauma, surgeries, skin grafts, physical therapy, wound care, emotional rollercoasters, doctor visits, casting for my prosthetic, etc., the time has come to stand again. I've never been so excited in my life and nervous all at the same time. I had the spirit of a kid and was just filled with joy and excitement. My emotions were running so high that it filled my whole body from my head to my feet. As I sat there waiting for the doctor to bring in my prosthetic, I look at myself in the mirror and tears flow from my eyes. Not tears of sadness but joy, so much joy in this much needed moment. I'm thinking of having no more wheelchair, no more crutches, no more using only my upper body strength to do everything. I couldn't see into the future, but I promised myself then that I was going to put my all into taking proper care of my prosthetic. I would diligently practice day in and day out with this new leg. Mentally, I had already made a plan to succeed and not give up or give in no matter what difficulties I faced.

The leg is placed on, and I roll up to the walkway in the office. Excitedly, I grab the rails with both hands. No lie, I felt like God came down as I began to stand up. His presence filled the room, and I felt him right there with me, encouraging me. I felt so light on my feet, and it just felt amazing to be standing straight up again on both legs. Four-and-a-half months later, and today, I stand on two legs. I was so excited that I didn't hear the first few words the doctor spoke. My mind was just overwhelmed, and my heart was filled with love and joy. As I made my first steps, Oh man, did it feel good. Felt so good I took another and another and another. Me, being me, I start to show off a bit. I bend my knees a little, dance a little, start doing a one-step – not totally able to do the two-step just yet. Then reality hit, that leg got tired really quick, and fatigue ran through my whole body. Suddenly, I had to sit back down to take a break. Nothing else mattered at this point, I was just glad I had my leg, and the doctor said I could leave with it today. Before leaving, he gave me instructions to follow and guidance to ensure that as I practice I don't overdo it and become unsafe.

Leaving that appointment rolling in my wheelchair, I still had a smile on my face because I have my prosthetic leg on also. This time, for the first time in a long time, I wasn't sitting looking at one leg with wonders of when the other would join, but now I was rolling with 2 legs wondering when I would retire this wheelchair for a while. Being an amputee is my new normal, and I was ready to put the work in to walk again, so I thought my first few days should be very rigorous on my body. Sometimes, my leg felts so heavy I didn't even think I could move. Up and down, up and down, I walked at home. Practicing putting one step ahead of the other, day in and day out. Practice really does help with any situation that is new or unfamiliar to you. I was in a position where I had to put my trust in using a prosthetic to walk up-right when I've had my leg for thirty-four years now. Let me tell you, it's a scary feeling and something that really takes patience and practice. My resolve to never give up no matter what I felt mentally finally came into play the day I was walking around with no assistance of a walker, cane, crutch, etc. Now don't get me wrong, I spent plenty of time putting in the work by walking inside and outside my home. This involved going to the store and having my family park a good distance away from the building so I could have a good distance to walk in. I would go to supermarkets and make myself walk through them as I grocery shopped. Some days I would walk with my walker, some days with my cane, many days leaning on the cart slow, stepping, and many days walking to entrance then using the wheelchairs or electric carts. I had to block out all the embarrassed feelings of everybody watching me and replace those with inner thoughts of you can do this, you came this far, keep pushing, keep going, only success will come from all of this.

10

Walk Before You Run

~

Walk Before You Run

Left, left right, left, left, left right left. I've put in the work to walk upright over a long period. I've reached success, some may say, but I don't want to stop there. Now during this time period from my accident day to the day I started walking again, my height has been up and down. Before the accident, I had started exercising regularly and was able to shed over one hundred pounds over a few years' time. I've never been a slim guy, but I was happy with my progress. Working out and being healthy was more of a lifestyle choice for me than a must, or a need to do. While in the hospital, I lost weight due to all the surgeries and not being able to eat hours prior to each procedures. Added to this, my lack of appetite from my spirit and pain level caused me to shed more pounds. Then once I became more settled, I gained it all back and plenty more after not being able to stand up or walk or jog around. Also because I had periods of being depressed, I would fill the void with food and laziness. *Well, that changes now*, I told myself,

I've had my prosthetic about four months now, and I'm not happy with the way I look so my journey to weight loss begins. Back in the gym, I started working my total body now. This involved many walks on the treadmill and elliptical. Being driven to continue to push myself, I decided that now I wanted to challenge myself and run again. Everything is different for me, but nothing is impossible. Even if it seems that way, sometimes you have to stop and say okay, *how can I achieve this now in my current state?*

One step at a time turns into a very slow job, and it begins . You see, you can't base success off of what you see others do , you must base it off of your own abilities, talents, and circumstances. Just like anything else, all this doesn't happen overnight, and as soon as you think nothing can stop you, think again.

My leg begins to hurt real bad with this added exercise, and at times, I felt like I couldn't move freely at all using my prosthetic. I was doing so good and kept pushing and pushing not taking time to slow down and make sure proper care was being taken for my leg. When you get excited, at times, you overlook possible problems that may arise in front of you. Now I'm dealing with leg swelling, sores, and joint pain around my hip area from pushing myself too hard, too fast. Not going to lie, it tore me up to know I was doing so well, and now I have to stop until it's time to start over again. Dealing with my amputation, I've learned that anything can send you into depression, that my-life-sucks mood, that I-will-never-be-normal mood, that why-me mood, that I-can't mood. But through it all, you have to remember where you started from and where you are now. Take time to reflect on how far you've come. Remember all the ups and downs before that didn't hinder what you thought to be your greatest moments so that means there's more great moments to come. Sometimes we need to stop, rest, recover, re-focus, and then start again to be able to push past where we thought we were. So here we go again, left, left, left, left, right left.

11

Just the Beginning

~

Just the Beginning

No matter what you do or how much you try to prepare yourself to live your absolute best life; there can be issues or problems that arise that will turn your world upside down. Religion was and is the driving force behind my acceptance of and recover from the traumatic accident that led to the amputation of my leg. The fear and uncertainty of life threatened to bring me into a pit of despair and leave me there to wallow in self-pity. At times, it seemed that no one understands. I'm sure that fellow victims have similar sentiments to mine. Anyone that has gone through a trauma will find that people are often sympathetic towards you, but they will never fully understand your emotions and ways of thinking. Even if they have had a similar incident occur in their life, each person's experience is still unique. Remember, everyone's comeback will not be the same, and it may not take the same amount of time. The biggest lesson I've learned through my trials is that not all will complete their comeback in their physical or mental state. The important thing is to just fight and have faith that each day you will make effort towards a comeback. Also I've learned you really have to keep faith and trust God and love yourself completely, no matter what you go through or have been through. I'll be the first to say that my faith has been, and still is being, tested. In my weak moments, I have cried out, "Lord, how much more?"

During this time, I also got to a place where I hated my physical body. This did not happen overnight; instead, it began with slow internal whispers that grew louder once I entertained their words. Over time, I reached the point where I lost love for myself, and it made the recover process harder to deal with. People will be people in that they will be there for you to encourage you. Meaning well, they can say all the right things that they think you need to hear, but no matter how well-intentioned they may be, they can never fully understand your situation. In the end, you have the choice in how you react to whatever happens to you in your life. You must understand these things in order to have that everlasting effect on our world. Through it all, you are a blessing regardless of what obstacles you may think you have. Also, God has given you unique abilities that he wants to use for to perform his will. He has promised and ensured that you have the strength to persevere and the ability to make a difference. Keep in mind that your life affects other's whether this be for an inspiration or a warning to others, your life matters. Just because you cannot do things exactly the same as you did before, you can find ways to get the same things done. Sometimes you have to stop, take a moment and think, take a step back and then push forward. In life, I've had to take a few steps back seemingly regressing in my progress, but I look at it as a necessary step in order to make my leap forward. So remember, no matter how many steps you have to take backwards, prepare yourself for that big leap forward that is sure to come. Understand that life will not be perfect or without bumps in the road. For me, I'm confident that there are more trials and tribulations coming in the future, but I know that when The Devil Knocks, God Answers!

12

Acknowledgements

- God, First Responders, Bystanders, Prayer Warriors, Individuals responsible for the tourniquet at the scene
- Hospital Staff & Trauma Unit at Memorial Hospital
- Gwen & Doctors & Staff at the University of Augusta Hospital
- Sabrina & Doctors & Staff at Candler Wound Care Center
- Ryan & Staff at the Mobility Institute at Memorial Hospital
- All the doctor's offices and staff that I've had appointments with through this process (too many to list individually)
- Jesse & Publix Company (especially my team at 1256)
- Sabrina & Kroger Company (especially Berwick Marketplace)
- Family- Erica Bryant, Henry Sr. & Alberta Bryant, Michael Bryant, Dwayne & Veronica Bryant, Janet & Jackie Bryant, Michael & Stephanie Kingston, Kenyada Moultrie, Vernice Moultrie,
- Frank & Mae Kyles, Chuckie, Bubba, Gubbie, and everyone that visited, called, donated, and prayed for God's healing grace.
- Friends – I thank you all each and every day, and you will never know how much your actions meant to me. From conversations and concerns from Travoya, jokes and laughs from Rob (Panda) /Melissa to Go Fund Me start-ups by Cassie. Thanks for all the

Facebook shares by Kesha and postings; donations and motivational words of support from you all (You know who you are!).

This book could not have been possible without the cover design by Ronnie Wreath, who brought my vision to life, and Melissa Zraik, who edited and provided her insights on how to improve the book further.

This is the start of many products, and I will continue to be an inspiration not only to myself but to others also. Love you all for all you and are doing in support of my new life situation/events.

13

Synopsis

The Devil Knocks, But God Answers came about from the traumatic motorcycle accident that I was involved in that resulted in serious pain, heartbreak, along with physical, emotional, spiritual, and psychological damage that ultimately resulted in the amputation of my right leg below the knee. I want to take you on a journey of my experience from that day to the day I received my prosthetic leg to be able to walk again. This scenario is told from my viewpoint through this process although I had supporters around me. You will be able to witness the events that caused my life-long change and my new relationship with the Amputee community. I want this book to inspire and motivate those who are going or have gone through an amputation and felt like they were alone. I never knew anyone with a prosthetic, nor was I around anyone for an extended period before I was faced with this myself. In the blink of an eye; I was on my way to this very lifestyle and unknown process and expectations. From my daily encounters, my story seems to be inspiring others regardless of challenges they have faced. This is the start of accepting my path in life and trying to share my story to help someone else.

FIVE TOES DOWN LLC

Henry Bryant